Blue Banner Biography

PINK

Mary Boone

WITHDRAWN

Mitchell Lane

P.O. Box 196
Hockessin, Delaware 19707
Visit us on the web: www.mitchelllane.com
Comments? email us: mitchelllane@mitchelllane.com

Printing   1   2   3   4   5   6   7   8   9

Blue Banner Biographies

Akon	Alan Jackson	Alicia Keys
Allen Iverson	Ashanti	Ashlee Simpson
Ashton Kutcher	Avril Lavigne	Bernie Mac
Beyoncé	Bow Wow	Brett Favre
Britney Spears	Carrie Underwood	Chris Brown
Chris Daughtry	Christina Aguilera	Christopher Paul Curtis
Ciara	Clay Aiken	Cole Hamels
Condoleezza Rice	Corbin Bleu	Daniel Radcliffe
David Ortiz	Derek Jeter	Eminem
Eve	Fergie (Stacy Ferguson)	50 Cent
Gwen Stefani	Ice Cube	Jamie Foxx
Joe Flacco	John Legend	Ja Rule
Jay-Z	Jennifer Lopez	Jessica Simpson
J. K. Rowling	Johnny Depp	JoJo
Justin Berfield	Justin Timberlake	Kanye West
Kate Hudson	Keith Urban	Kelly Clarkson
Kenny Chesney	Kristen Stewart	Lance Armstrong
Leona Lewis	Lil Wayne	Lindsay Lohan
Mariah Carey	Mario	Mary J. Blige
Mary-Kate and Ashley Olsen	Miguel Tejada	Missy Elliott
Nancy Pelosi	Natasha Bedingfield	Nelly
Orlando Bloom	P. Diddy	Paris Hilton
Peyton Manning	Pink	Queen Latifah
Rihanna	Ron Howard	Rudy Giuliani
Sally Field	Sean Kingston	Selena
Shakira	Shontelle Layne	Soulja Boy Tell 'Em
Taylor Swift	T.I.	Timbaland
Tim McGraw	Toby Keith	Usher
Vanessa Anne Hudgens	Zac Efron	

Library of Congress Cataloging-in-Publication Data
Boone, Mary, 1963–
  Pink / by Mary Boone.
    p. cm. — (Blue banner biographies)
  Includes bibliographical references and index.
  ISBN 978-1-58415-767-0 (library bound)
  1. Pink, 1979– —Juvenile literature. 2. Singers—United States—Biography—Juvenile literature.
I. Title.
  ML3930.P467B66 2009
  782.42164092—dc22
  [B]

2009006304

ABOUT THE AUTHOR: Mary Boone has written thirteen books for young adults, including Blue Banner Biographies about Akon, 50 Cent, Corbin Bleu, and Vanessa Hudgens. Boone lives in Tacoma, Washington, where she enjoys running, swimming, and being outdoors with her husband, Mitch, their two children, Eve and Eli, and their dog, Iris.

PUBLISHER'S NOTE: The following story has been thoroughly researched, and to the best of our knowledge represents a true story. While every possible effort has been made to ensure accuracy, the publisher will not assume liability for damages caused by inaccuracies in the data and makes no warranty on the accuracy of the information contained herein. This story has not been authorized or endorsed by Alecia Moore/Pink.

Blue Banner Biography

Pink and her father, James Moore, attend the 2000 Billboard Music Awards, where Pink was honored as New Female Artist of the Year.

Musical Beginnings

Superstar Pink can't help getting teary when she looks at photos from the 2000 Billboard Music Awards. Sure, she was delighted to be named New Female Artist of the Year. But her real thrill came because she was able to take her father as her date to the awards show.

"He used to take me to Vietnam vet chapter meetings and we would play guitar and sing songs and I felt like a little superstar," she told *Interview* magazine. "That made me want to make music, because I was a really bad kid, so I was like, 'Let me just make him proud.'

"I saw a picture of us [at the awards show] and it's the proudest I've ever seen him look. That will make me cry every time I look at the picture. That, to me, is triumph."

Pink, named Alecia Beth Moore by her parents, James Jr. and Judy Moore, was born September 8, 1979. She grew up in Doylestown, Pennsylvania, a town of about 8,000 people just north of Philadelphia.

Rumors regarding the origins of Pink's nickname abound. Some suggest she got it because her cheeks turned pink when she first began performing. There are those who insist the name comes from Mr. Pink, a character in Quentin Tarantino's 1992 film *Reservoir Dogs*. Others say the nickname is related to the embarrassment she suffered when a boy pulled down her pants at summer camp. While unwilling to confirm any of these theories, Pink (also spelled P!nk) only says she's had the nickname since she was a little girl—long before she first dyed her hair pink.

Pink's wild and varied youth included recording her first original song by the time she was fourteen.

Some of Pink's earliest memories are of listening to her mother's music collection, including records by Aretha Franklin, Dionne Warwick, Shirley Murdock, and Donny Hathaway. Her father, a talented guitarist, introduced her to the music of Janis Joplin, Bob Dylan, the Mamas and the Papas, and Billy Joel. Their love of good music was infectious.

A self-described "wild child," Pink told Launch Media's Billy Johnson Jr.: "I was into everything. I didn't think there was one thing you couldn't do. At the same time I was singing gospel in church, I was the lead singer of a rock band. I was going to rave clubs, going to hip-hop clubs, going to school, playing field hockey and gymnastics, skateboarding, whatever. I just did everything. I was everywhere. I thought I was 30 when I was 10."

Pink's wild and varied youth included recording her first original song by the time she was fourteen. A year later, she landed a regular singing gig at a hip-hop club. Shortly after that, she became lead singer of a girl group called Basic Instinct. Her bandmates soon voted her out of the group

Judy Moore and Pink hang out at New York City's Beacon Theatre in 2002. Judy's love of rhythm and blues was an early influence on her daughter.

"because they were black and I was white," she told *Interview*, "but the politically correct reason that they gave me was because I didn't fit in well in the photos."

Through it all, Pink's parents divorced, and Pink dropped out of high school, did drugs, got arrested for trespassing and petty theft, was kicked out of her house, and worked at a score of minimum-wage jobs for such businesses as Pizza Hut, McDonald's, Wendy's, and a gas station.

When she was sixteen, Pink became lead singer for a rhythm and blues group called Choice. The band signed a record deal with La Face Records but disbanded before they were able to record anything.

The band's bad luck turned out to be Pink's good fortune. She so impressed La Face label executives that they decided to take her on as a solo artist.

"I went from staying up all night and sleeping all day to getting up early, running, getting in shape, getting my lungs right, getting my mind right, singing, practicing eight hours a day," she told Launch Media.

The hard work paid off. Pink's raspy voice, unexpected style, and outspoken ways have helped her outlast many of her contemporaries.

"I don't try to be candy-coated," she told Launch. "I don't try to walk on eggshells. I am what I am. Love me or hate me."

> When she was sixteen, Pink became lead singer for a rhythm and blues group called Choice. The band signed a record deal with La Face Records . . .

Hitting the Big Time

*P*ink recorded her debut album, *Can't Take Me Home,* with the help of a variety of songwriting partners and producers. Released in April 2000, the album earned multiplatinum status (more than 2 million copies sold) and yielded three Top Ten singles: "There U Go," "Most Girls," and "You Make Me Sick."

Buoyed by the CD's success, Pink went on a summer 2000 tour as the opening act for 'N Sync. She quickly tired of the show's highly produced format and disliked being labeled as a "teen" act. It was enough to send her back to the studio to work on her follow-up album.

While she was writing and recording, Pink took a short break from her solo work to record a remake of Patti LaBelle's "Lady Marmalade" with Christina Aguilera, Mya, and Lil' Kim. The song, featured on the *Moulin Rouge Soundtrack,* went to number one in both the United States and United Kingdom. An accompanying cabaret-style video placed number three on MTV's *Total Request Live* year-end countdown and exposed Pink to a whole new audience.

Pink's follow-up CD, *M!ssundaztood*, was released in November 2001. It also earned multiplatinum sales, selling more than 5.2 million copies in the United States. Her single "Get the Party Started" climbed into the Top Five and became a dance-club favorite. "Don't Let Me Get Me" became another fast-rising Top 10 hit. The CD—named to *Rolling Stone*'s list of the 50 Best Albums of 2002—was both a commercial and critical success that demonstrated a raw edginess not evident on Pink's more mainstream debut.

Pink's pooch accompanies her to the 2001 MTV Movie Awards, where Pink, Lil' Kim, Mya, and Christina Aguilera performed "Lady Marmalade" live. Pink has a passion for animals, and advocates against animal cruelty.

Entertainment Weekly music critic Jim Farber rated the CD an "A-" and wrote: "While the 22-year-old's 2000 debut *Can't Take Me Home* introduced her as the white Destiny's Child, her follow-up, *M!ssundaztood*, makes her sound like Cyndi Lauper's long lost stepsister. It's a fetching collection of pop confections, lacking even a hint of the clichéd R&B that made earlier Pink songs like 'Most Girls' and 'You Make Me Sick' into hits."

Stephen Thomas Erlewine of *All Music Guide* said of the album: "There hasn't been a record in the mainstream this vibrant or this alive in a long, long time."

Pink's next album, *Try This*, was released in November 2003. Through the project, Pink took a giant step toward a more punk-rock sound. The CD's lead single, "Trouble," cracked the *Billboard* Top 40 and was featured in the film *White Chicks*. It also earned Pink a Grammy award for Best Female Rock Vocal Performance and spawned an extensive European tour. Despite its many successes, the album never really connected with the record-buying public; only 700,000 copies sold in the United States. Pink insists the dismal sales don't mean the album was a failure. Rather, it gave her a much-needed opportunity to stretch in new directions.

> **Pink's next album, *Try This*, was released in November 2003. Through the project, Pink took a giant step toward a more punk-rock sound.**

"*Try This* was my rebellion against deadlines," she told *Billboard*. "Fine, you want your . . . records. I'll write 10 songs in a week, and you can press it and put it out. I don't have to think about it. I don't have to get emotionally invested. . . . I

Pink flashes her diamond engagement ring. She and Carey Hart married in 2006, after four years of dating. Pink proposed to Hart during one of his motocross races. She stood in the pit, holding a sign that read: "Will you marry me?" On the other side was written, "I'm serious!"

walked out of half of my interviews crying. I needed to coast for a while, and that's what I did."

"Coasting" for Pink meant taking time for herself. She married her longtime boyfriend, motocross star Carey Hart, whom she had met at 2001's X Games. She slept in, traveled, and spent time with her dogs. Then—when she was ready— she went back to the studio to make the kind of album she really wanted to make.

Stupid Girls and Lost Love

*P*ink took a three-year hiatus before releasing her third album, *I'm Not Dead*. The CD's first single—the confrontational tune "Stupid Girls"—became a quick hit, and its accompanying video was all over MTV. The song pokes fun at ultra-thin, blond celebrities, including Paris Hilton, Mary-Kate Olsen, Lindsay Lohan, and Jessica Simpson. It humorously ridicules breast implants, spray-on tans, and eating disorders.

Pink shot the "Stupid Girls" video with her longtime collaborator Dave Meyers. "I love making videos and I love making videos with Dave Meyers. He just gets it," she told *Entertainment Weekly*. "I like to be physical and do my own stunts and he allows for that. He has an insane imagination. I don't think anyone ever stopped laughing during 'Stupid Girl' [sic]. I don't think everyone else is going to laugh, but just know that we all did."

Doing her own stunts is not without risk. Pink got injured during the "Stupid Girls" video shoot, chipping a bone in her wrist and cutting her thigh when she fell off a car. The pain, however, subsided as the video soared in

Pink performs at a release party for I'm Not Dead. *The talented musician produced and wrote or cowrote every song on the CD.*

popularity, garnering praise from critics and the public—except, perhaps, from the young starlets it mocked.

"I never heard from any of them," Pink told *Entertainment Weekly.* "But before the video came out we heard from a couple of publicists. Just 'Call me back right now, I want an advance copy of this thing.' "

Not surprisingly, Pink ignored the publicists' requests.

"U + Ur Hand" is another notable single from *I'm Not Dead.* The infectious track pokes fun at men who—unsuccessfully—try to meet women in nightclubs. It debuted on the Hot 100 at number 94 and peaked at number 9. The single also enjoyed great success in Europe: It reached number one in the United Kingdom, number four in Germany, and number one in France.

In the end, *I'm Not Dead* generated seven singles and sold more than 6 million copies worldwide, pumping up excitement for Pink's follow-up, *Funhouse.* It was released in October 2008.

> *In the end, I'm Not Dead generated seven singles and sold more than 6 million copies worldwide, pumping up excitement for Pink's follow-up, Funhouse.*

Pink calls *Funhouse* her most vulnerable album to date. Several songs on the disc focus on her breakup with Hart, and the range of emotions the heartbreak has evoked. "So What," the album's leadoff single, has a pulsating beat and generally optimistic outlook:

I guess I just lost my husband, I don't know where he went.
So I'm gonna drink my money, I'm not gonna pay his rent.
I got a brand new attitude, and I'm gonna wear it tonight.
I'm gonna get in trouble. I wanna start a fight.

Pink celebrates the release of her fifth studio album, Funhouse, *in London in 2008. The album's first single, "So What," was the biggest solo success of her career to that point.*

The single — with a chorus that proclaims "So what, I'm still a rock star" — became Pink's first number one hit since "Lady Marmalade." The accompanying video garnered considerable press, largely because Hart appeared in it.

"Carey hadn't even heard the song before he did the video," Pink wrote on her official web site. "That's how much he loves and trusts me. He pretty much just rolls his eyes, throws his hands up in the air and hugs me. He gets it. He gets me. It's nice."

Funhouse's disco-infused title track tells of burning down the house she once shared with her husband. "Sober" is a rocking song about the vices people use to forget their problems. Fans get a look at Pink's more vulnerable side in tracks like "I Don't Believe You" and "Please Don't Leave Me."

Writing and singing about her breakup was therapeutic for Pink. "It's like letting down the armor and admitting I'm human, I'm a girl," she wrote on her web site. "We all want to be loved and love. That's all we want."

Of course, the whole album isn't about heartbreak. There are also cuts about girls having fun ("Bad Influence"), drugs ("One Foot Wrong"), and the world's social issues ("Ave Mary A").

With its mix of acoustic guitar ballads and rollicking rock, Pink seems to have accomplished her goals with *Funhouse*. The album touches on mostly tender topics, interspersing deep emotion with Pink's irreverent sense of humor.

> *Writing and singing about her breakup was therapeutic for Pink. "It's like letting down the armor and admitting I'm human, I'm a girl."*

Creative Collaboration

*P*ink's star shines bright when she performs solo. She becomes a supernova when she teams up with other musicians.

The artist had won her first Grammy award in 2001, when she collaborated with Christina Aguilera, Lil' Kim, and Mya on "Lady Marmalade." Produced by hip-hop legends Rockwilder and Missy Elliott, the massive hit helped to expand Pink's audience.

Teaming up with former 4 Non Blondes singer Linda Perry later that year further energized Pink. The two wrote and rocked together, and the result was Pink's multiplatinum album *M!ssundaztood*.

Perry says when she got Pink's call, she initially thought it might be a wrong number.

"I thought she was nuts to call me up. I'd never heard of her before," Perry told *Playback Magazine*. At the time, Perry was preparing to record her own album and even had a showcase scheduled with a handful of record label executives. "I called up my manager and said, 'Cancel the

Pink performs with Mya, Lil' Kim, and Christina Aguilera at the 2001 MTV Video Music Awards. The four musicians nabbed the trophy for Video of the Year.

showcase. I'm gonna go investigate this girl. There's something here. I have a gut feeling.' "

Perry agreed to produce for, cowrite, and perform with Pink. The partnership resulted in a handful of hits, including "Let's Get This Party Started," "Don't Let Me Get Me," and "Lonely Girl."

Following the success of *M!ssundaztood*, Pink issued *Try This* in November 2003. The CD continued her progression toward more rock-oriented material, due in part to her collaboration with songwriter/singer Tim Armstrong. The two cowrote eight of the album's tracks, including the lead single, "Trouble." On *I'm Not Dead,* Pink teamed up with hit-makers Billy Mann (of Backstreet Boys fame) and Max Martin (Britney Spears's go-to guy).

Throughout her career, Pink has continued to perform, write, and record with other artists.

The Indigo Girls—Amy Ray and Emily Saliers—performed with Pink on her single "Dear Mr. President." In 2006, she returned the favor, recording "Rock and Roll Heaven's Gate," with the Indigo Girls for their *Despite Our Differences* CD.

> *"I think when you bring creative people together, it doesn't matter what their genre is, it works," said Saliers.*

"You could write a song and right away think that it needs another voice," Saliers told Express Milwaukee.com. "It was like that with Pink. We said, 'Pink would be great on this song; let's ask her.' We had sung on her record, so we asked her to sing on ours."

The folksy Indigo Girls and pop-rock oriented Pink may not seem to be a natural pairing, but Saliers says blending genres often results in musical magic. "It's just more exciting to pull someone from a whole different walk of life into your music to see what happens," she said. "More often than not, there's a chemistry there that you couldn't have anticipated. I think a lot of people think of Pink as a pop star, but she has such a range. She can do anything—blues, acoustic music, rock, hip-hop or whatever she wanted. I think when you bring creative people together, it doesn't matter what their genre is, it works. Things can come together that can really blow your mind."

Pink kicked off her Funhouse *tour in Belgium in February 2009. Her onstage antics — and music — were widely praised by critics.*

The list of artists with whom Pink has worked is long and diverse, including names such as soul singer India Arie, pop star Hilary Duff, Spanish singer Natalia, R&B artist Kenny "Babyface" Edmonds, Scottish legend Annie Lennox, and country songstress Faith Hill. She has even collaborated with her dad, James Moore. The two recorded a duet of "I Have Seen the Rain," an antiwar tune James wrote while serving in Vietnam; it's the hidden track on *I'm Not Dead.*

"It was the first song I ever learned," Pink told *Entertainment Weekly.* "I used to tell [my dad] three things: I'm going to be famous, we're going to record this song, and I'm going to buy you a motor home. Every Christmas card, I wrote, 'Motor home's coming soon.' "

Going to a Pink concert is sometimes like watching a circus. Her 2009 Funhouse tour was big and loud with onstage slides, dancers, acrobats, giant inflatable clowns, and plenty of costume changes.

Pink has, of course, found fame. And she recorded her dad's song.

What about the motor home?

"He doesn't want it anymore," she told *Entertainment Weekly*. "I'm like, 'What . . . ?' I *have* to complete the dream. It's not about *you*. Ha!"

Not Afraid to Take a Stand

*P*ink has used her music to share her unwavering opinions about topics ranging from animal abuse and girls' self-esteem to war and politics. In the 2001 single "Respect," for instance, she sings:

> *Hey ladies*
> *Let 'em know it ain't easy*
> *R-E-S-P-E-C-T*

Not even the U.S. president is safe from Pink's lyrical opining. Her 2007 release "Dear Mr. President" is a harsh indictment of George W. Bush, who was president at the time. Pink wrote the tune with Billy Mann. In concert, Pink sings with video of the war in Iraq and Hurricane Katrina as the visual backdrop, just to make sure no one wonders what—or whom—she's talking about:

> *How can you say no child is left behind? We're not dumb and we're not blind.*
> *They're all sitting in your cells, while you pave the road to hell.*
> *What kind of father would take his own daughter's rights away?*
> *And what kind of father would hate his own daughter if she were gay?*

"This is one of the smarter songs I've ever written," Pink told *Billboard* magazine. "My way is usually waving the flag and saying, 'You're wrong, burn in hell.' This is subtle and provocative, and it's very innocent. "

Aware that her song might offend radio advertisers and, consequently, be pulled from the air, Pink spent her own money to buy airtime so that "Dear Mr. President" could be played on major radio stations across the country.

Pink says her intent is not to randomly insult and disparage. Instead, she hopes to inspire dialogue and raise awareness.

"I don't pick a different group to trash [in] each song. Most of the time, I'm just trashing myself," she told *Billboard*.

> *While many other artists avoid controversy so as not to offend fans, Pink insists she won't stay quiet just so she can make more money.*

While many other artists avoid controversy so as not to offend fans, Pink insists she won't stay quiet just so she can make more money.

"There's definitely a neutral trend happening," she told Australia's *Herald Sun*. That's very successful for most people. People in America particularly don't like my sarcasm. But it ain't going to go away—nor am I."

Music is not the only means by which Pink has made her opinions known. She has become an outspoken campaigner for PETA (People for the Ethical Treatment of Animals), lending her star power to many of the group's campaigns, including a protest of horse-drawn carriages, a boycott of Australian wool, and a protest against KFC restaurants. PETA's web site also salutes Pink for criticizing singer Beyoncé for wearing fur, and for writing letters to England's Prince William for his support of fox hunting and to Queen Elizabeth II for continuing to allow bear fur to be used on her guards' caps. In January 2007, she headlined a benefit concert in Cardiff, Wales. The event, called PAW (Party for Animals Worldwide), highlighted her work against animal cruelty.

Pink contributes to and has done work on behalf of dozens of charitable organizations, some of which include the Human Rights Campaign (which works to ensure equal rights for lesbian, gay, bisexual, and transgender individuals), ONE Campaign (an effort to fight AIDS and poverty), Prince's Trust (which provides money and support to help

Pink generously gives both time and money to a variety of charitable organizations, including the Breast Cancer Research Foundation.

people start businesses), New York Restoration Project (which creates and restores parks and community gardens), Run for the Cure Foundation (which funds education and awareness about breast cancer in Japan), and Save the Children (which works to create lasting change for disadvantaged children in forty-two nations).

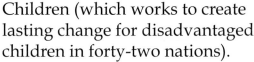

Speaking her mind—whether it's about peace or pets, politics or cancer prevention—is something Pink is happy to do.

After Barack Obama took office in January 2009, rumors surfaced that Pink was working with producer Damon Elliott and singer Macy Gray to produce a peace-oriented charity tune called "Stomp for Change."

"It's based on the positive attitude that [President] Obama has set forth," Damon told *Life & Style* magazine. "It's been a long time since there was a 'We Are the World' type song that will hopefully have such a positive message."

"We Are the World" was a huge hit in 1985 for USA for Africa. The song, written by Michael Jackson and Lionel Richie, was recorded by a group of superstars including Stevie Wonder, Paul Simon, Kenny Rogers, and Tina Turner. That single raised funds to help famine-relief efforts in Ethiopia.

Speaking her mind—whether it's about peace or pets, politics or cancer prevention—is something Pink is happy to do. She often takes breaks during live performances and TV interviews to share her thoughts about a particular social cause.

"I'm just more aware," she told Knight Ridder Newspapers. "There's so much happening in the world, so many reasons to take the blinders off."

Pink stops by Fuse Studios in October 2008 to meet with children from the Starlight Foundation. The foundation is devoted to brightening the lives of seriously ill and hospitalized children.

Pink promises to continue to use her stardom to give a voice to those who might not otherwise be heard. It's a trait that has earned her a loyal following of fans who respect both her strong voice and her strong opinions.

1979	Born Alecia Beth Moore on September 8, in Doylestown, Pennsylvania, to James and Judy Moore
1992	Begins singing with a gospel choir
1993	Starts singing with a local punk band and records her first original song
1996	NBC announces she'll sing the theme music for its Sunday night NFL broadcasts
2000	Releases debut album *Can't Take Me Home*; tours with 'N Sync
2001	Releases *M!ssundaztood*
2002	Ranks 36th in *Stuff* magazine's list of "102 Sexiest Women in the World"
2003	Has a cameo role in and contributes a song to the feature film *Charlie's Angels: Full Throttle*; releases her third album, *Try This*
2004	Stars in a Pepsi commercial with Britney Spears, Beyoncé, and Enrique Iglesias
2006	Marries motocross racer Carey Hart in Costa Rica; issues her fourth album, *I'm Not Dead*
2007	Appears in the horror film *Catacombs*
2008	Announces her separation from Hart; releases *Funhouse*, including the immediate hit single "So What"
2009	*Funhouse* tour begins in France on February 23

DISCOGRAPHY

Albums

2008	*Funhouse*
2006	*I'm Not Dead*
2003	*Try This*
2001	*M!ssundaztood*
2000	*Can't Take Me Home*

Soundtrack Contributions/Compilations

2009	*2009 Grammy Nominees*
2008	*Now That's What I Call Music! 29*
	The Best of Now That's What I call Music! 10th Anniversary
	2008 Rock Camp Studio Showcase
2007	*Ultra 2008*
	Now That's What I Call Music! 26
	The Hills – The Soundtrack
	Now That's What I Call Music! 25
	Ultra Weekend 3
	Thrivemix Presents Dance Anthems
	Rhapsody Presents 2007 Clive Davis Pre-Grammy Show Vol. 1
	2007 Grammy Nominees
	Now That's What I Call Music Vol. 64
	L Tunes: Music from and Inspired by "The L Word"
2006	*Music from the Motion Picture "Happy Feet"*
	Mean Girls – Original Soundtrack
2005	*Voices*
	Superstars #1 Hits Remixed
	Love Rocks
2004	*Lizzie McGuire: Total Party!*
	The Princess Diaries 2
2003	*Charlie's Angels: Full Throttle*
	Ultimate Smash Hits
	Hit List! Vol. 9: The Best of January 2003
2002	*Hit List! Vol. 8: The Best of December 2002*
	Totally Hits 2002
2001	*MTV Party to Go (remixed)*
2000	*La Face Records Presents the Platinum Collection*
	Vibe Hits, Vol. 1
	Totally Hits, Vol. 3
	Music from the Motion Picture "Save the Last Dance"
	Ultimate Dance Party 2000

FILMOGRAPHY

2007   *Catacombs*
2003   *Charlie's Angels: Full Throttle*
2002   *Rollerball*

AWARDS

2009   Grammy nomination for Best Female Pop Vocal Performance for "So What"; BRIT (British Record Industry Trust) Award nomination for Best International Female Artist

2008   MTV Australia Music Award for Best Live Performer for *I'm Not Dead* tour; MTV Europe Music Award for Most Addictive Track for "So What"; World Music Award nomination for World's Best Pop/Rock Female Artist

2007   Grammy nomination for Best Female Pop Vocal Performance for "Stupid Girls"; BRIT Award nomination for Best International Female Artist; MTV Australia Music Award nomination for Album of the Year for *I'm Not Dead*; MTV Australia Music Award for Download of the Year for "Who Knew"; MTV Australia Music Award for Best Female Artist for "U + Ur Hand"; MTV Australia Music Award nomination for Best Pop Video for "U + Ur Hand"

2004   Grammy Award for Best Female Rock Vocal Performance for "Trouble"; Grammy nomination for Best Pop Collaboration with Vocals for "Feel Good Time"

2003   Grammy nomination for Best Pop Vocal Performance for "Get the Party Started"; Grammy nomination for *M!ssundaztood*; BRIT Award for Best International Female Artist

2001   Grammy Award for Best Pop Collaboration with Vocals for "Lady Marmalade" (with Christina Aguilera, Lil' Kim, and Mya)

2000   Billboard Music Award for Best New Female Artist of the Year

FURTHER READING

Works Consulted

Cinquemani, Sal. "Pink: Try This." *Slant Magazine*, http://www.slantmagazine.com, 2003.

Collis, Clark. "The Upside of Anger: Pink Wants to Talk About 'Stupid Girls'—The Singer's New Video Mocks Lindsay Lohan, Paris Hilton, Jessica Simpson, and Mary-Kate Olsen." *Entertainment Weekly*, March 31, 2006.

Conniff, Tamara. "Think Pink: She Is a Complex Woman—Honest, Vulgar, Sweet, Intelligent, Hard and Vulnerable—Like Her Music." *Billboard*, March 11, 2006, pp. 22–23.

Erlewine, Stephen Thomas. "Pink: M!ssundaztood." *All Music Guide*, www.starpulse.com, 2001.

Farber, Jim. "Big Music From Pink." *Entertainment Weekly*, November 23, 2001, www.ew.com.

Farber, Jim. "Pink Has Bad News for Feminists: She Thinks the Movement Failed." Knight-Ridder Newspapers, May 13, 2006.

Hall, Rashaun. "Pink Insists She's 'M!ssundaztood.' " *Billboard*, November 30, 2001. www.billboard.com.

Johnson, Billy, Jr. "The Legendary Pink Talks." Launch Media, February 8, 2004, http://music.yahoo.com/read/interview/12028289

Manson, Shirley. "Pink: She Sings from the Heart and Speaks Her Mind." *Interview*, December 2001.

Moon, Jin. "Linda Perry: High Priestess of Pop." *Playback Magazine*, Fall 2003, www.ascap.com.

Rosenberg, Carissa. "Don't Let the Tough Shell Fool You—Her Heart Breaks Just Like the Rest of Ours." *Seventeen*, February 2009, pp. 88–93.

Thompson, Brent. "Twenty Years of the Indigo Girls." *Express Milwaukee*, June 4, 2008, www.expressmilwaukee.com.

Vineyard, Jennifer. "Pink Would Rather Fall Off a Car Than Get Glammed Up for Her Videos." MTV, December 21, 2005. http://www.mtv.com/news/articles/1519101/20051221/pink.jhtml

On the Internet

MTV: Pink
http://www.mtv.com/music/artist/pink/artist.jhtml

The Official Pink Site
http://www.pinkspage.com